Illustrations by Philip Watkins

FREDERICK MULLER LIMITED
LONDON.

Superted loves the countryside. He was out walking one day when he came across a little boy who was wandering alone near a deep, dark forest.

In a kind voice Superted asked, 'Why are you on your own? Isn't anyone looking after you?'

'I'm lost,' said the boy. 'My big brother and sister went inside Creepy Castle and didn't come out.'

'Where's Creepy Castle?' asked Superted.

'In the forest,' said the little boy, and started to cry.

'Don't cry,' said Superted. 'Have you ever flown before?'

'No,' said the little boy.

'Well, just close your eyes for one moment, and you'll have a surprise.'

Superted whispered his very secret magic word, which no one else knows, and stepped behind a tree. When the child opened his eyes he realized who he had been talking to, and stopped crying. Superted held his hand gently with his paw, then flew him up and away over the forest.

Soon they saw Creepy Castle, flew down, and landed by the huge front door. Superted rapped the door with his paw: Knock! Knock! Knock! No reply. He flew at the door at super speed. Bash! the door burst open.

The little boy, whose name was David, held on to Superted's paw as he looked inside the dark castle.

They walked inside and called the lost children's names: 'Christopher, Nicola, where are you?'

'Down here in the dungeon,' came the very faint reply. 'We are locked in. The door is made of iron bars.'

Superted found the dungeon and twisted the bars until there was enough room for the children to squeeze out.

'Who put you in there?' Superted asked.

'A big man dressed in black. He has two creepy monsters—one is called Bulk, and is very strong indeed, the other looks like a skeleton. We must get out of here quickly.'

Superted led the three children through the dark corridors until they were safely outside, then said, 'I'm going back to find out what this is all about.'

Zoom! He flew back in, and at super speed searched through all the rooms until he found the skeleton—who jumped up in front of him and said, 'Boo! Rattle! Boo!'

Superted was rather frightened, but, remembering who he was, grabbed the skeleton's bony leg, and turned him upside down.

'Ooow!' shouted the skeleton. Then suddenly a funny thing happened. The skeleton turned out to be a boy wearing a painted skeleton outfit.

'You wait here until I come back,' said Superted, hanging the boy by his collar on a hook on the wall.

OOOW!

Superted flew to the next dark room, turned on his special flashlight, and there he found the Bulk.

With a loud roar the monster charged at Superted, who twirled the Bulk over his head in a great somersault, landed him on his back and quickly sat on his chest. Superted pulled off the Bulk's mask and beneath found a fat young man who puffed, 'Get off me. You're squashing me.'

Superted said, 'You were only good at frightening children. Where's the man in black?'

'It's all his fault,' stammered the young man. 'He's a thief who keeps his stolen goods in this creepy castle and pays us to frighten people who come looking around.'

Just as Superted had tied up the young man he heard a car starting, and flew outside.

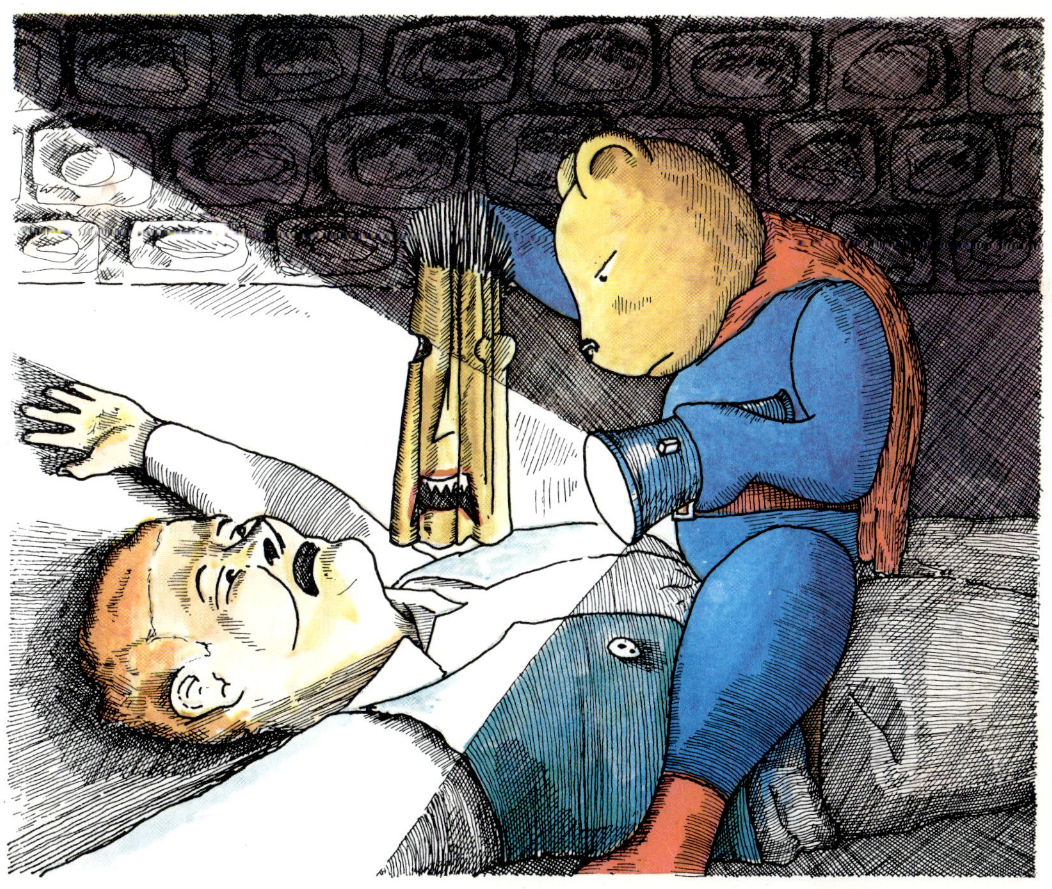

There was the man in black just escaping in a speedy red car.

Off flew Superted, and landed on the road in front of the car. 'Stop!' he said, holding up his right paw.

But the man in black said, 'I'm not stopping for any old teddy bear,' and drove straight at Superted.

Superted flew around to the back of the car, picked it up, and flew off to the nearest police station.

He quickly explained everything to the surprised policeman, then flew back to Creepy Castle.

POLICE

The policeman followed in his van to collect the silly boys who pretended to be the skeleton and Bulk.

'Right,' said Superted to the children. 'We are going home.'

The children squealed with excitement as they zoomed up into the sky.

Their mummy was so pleased at Superted's super rescue that she invited him to tea. Crisps, cakes and jelly.

Good eating, Superted.